Mysteries
OF THE
UNIVERSE

This edition published 2000
© Aladdin Books Ltd 2000
Original edition published 1995

Designed and produced by
Aladdin Books Ltd
28 Percy Street
London W1P 0LD

First Published in the United States by
Copper Beech Books, an imprint of
The Millbrook Press
2 Old New Milford Road
Brookfield, Connecticut 06804

Editor: Katie Roden
Design: David West Children's Book Design
Designer: Flick Killerby
Picture Research: Brooks Krikler Research
Illustrators: Ian Thompson,
Gary Slater, Simon Girling and Associates, Rob Shone.

Printed in Belgium

Library of Congress Cataloging-in-Publication Data

Hawkes, Nigel.
The universe / by Nigel Hawkes.
p. cm. -- (Mysteries of--)
Includes index.
ISBN 1-56294-939-X (lib. bdg.)
1-56294-195-X (pbk.)
1. Astronomy--Juvenile literature.
[1. Astronomy.] I. Title II. Series.
QB46.H27 1995   95-13396

Mysteries
OF THE
UNIVERSE

Nigel Hawkes

Copper Beech Books
Brookfield, Connecticut

VENUS
Rocky; liquid core
Diameter: 7,521 miles
Distance from Sun: 67 million miles
Number of moons: 0

MERCURY
Ball of rock; iron-rich core
Diameter: 3,030 miles
Distance from Sun: 36 million miles
Number of moons: 0

EARTH
Rocky ball; metallic core
Diameter: 7,926 miles
Distance from Sun: 93 million miles
Number of moons: 1

MARS
Rocky ball; iron-rich core
Diameter: 4,220 miles
Distance from Sun: 142 million miles
Number of moons: 2

JUPITER (right)
Gas and liquid gases; small rocky core
Diameter: 88,700 miles
Distance from Sun: 483 million miles
Number of moons: 16

SATURN
Gas and liquid gases; small rocky core
Diameter: 75,000 miles
Distance from Sun: 936 million miles
Number of moons: 18

NEPTUNE
Ball of gas; metal core
Diameter: 30,800 miles
Distance from Sun: 2,794 million miles
Number of moons: 8

PLUTO
Ball of rock and ice
Diameter: 1,800 miles
Distance from Sun: 3,660 million miles
Number of moons: 1

URANUS
Gas; rocky core
Diameter: 32,300 miles
Distance from Sun: 1,783 million miles
Number of moons: 15

CONTENTS

"Ever since the dawn of civilization, people have not been content to see events as unconnected and inexplicable... today we still yearn to know why we are here and where we came from. And our goal is nothing less than a complete description of the universe we live in."

Stephen Hawking,
A Brief History of Time

Introduction to THE MYSTERIES

The mysteries of the night sky have fascinated scientists, writers, artists, and many other people throughout history. Every civilization has tried to understand our universe, but although many great discoveries have been made, we are still a long way from knowing all its secrets. The twentieth century saw many enormous breakthroughs in the exploration of space, and new, more complex technology is constantly being created to help us fulfil our quest for knowledge.

Our universe is teeming with satellites, probes, and telescopes, all with one purpose – to unravel the tangled secrets of space. How, and when did the universe begin? Will we ever find life in other galaxies? Could black holes make time travel possible? Is there a tenth planet (Planet X) in our solar system? Will our universe get bigger and bigger until it eventually freezes, or will it shrink and collapse in a big crunch?

Perhaps one day we will know the answers to all these questions, and to the thousands more that have perplexed people for hundreds of years. For the moment, we can only try to reach deeper and deeper into the mysteries of our universe.

"The novelty of these things stirred up against me no small number of professors ... as if I had placed these things in the sky with my own hands in order to upset Nature and overturn science!"
Galileo Galilei

The Mysterious UNIVERSE

Galileo Galilei (1564–1642) was the first astronomer to look at the sky through a telescope. What he saw when he turned toward the planet Jupiter, on January 7, 1610, astonished him. "Four tiny little stars" were seen in close orbit. They were Jupiter's moons. Their discovery was a challenge to the Christian Church's belief that the Earth was the center of the universe. They proved that not everything moved around the Earth.

Other people before Galileo had the same idea, including the Polish priest Nicolaus Copernicus (1473–1543), but Galileo now had solid evidence. The Catholic Pope said the idea was "false and absurd." Galileo retired, but in 1632 published his support for Copernicus's ideas. He was summoned to the Pope and threatened with torture. He finally rejected his theory, but he muttered, "E pur si muove" ("And yet it does move"). He stayed under house arrest, unable to leave his home, until his death in 1642.

The First MYSTERIES

SUN WORSHIP
The ancient Egyptians believed that the sky was the goddess Nut (left), stretching her body over the Earth. They saw the Sun as the god Re (or Ra). When members of the royal family died, boats were often put in their tombs so that they could join Re on his heavenly journey.

Since the dawn of civilization, people have been fascinated by the mysteries of the heavens. The ancient Babylonians and Greeks were the first to divide the stars in the sky into groups called *constellations*, which are still used today. They also watched the movements of the planets, and recorded the arrival of comets and the behavior of supernovae (exploding stars). The Egyptian pyramids and the stone circle of Stonehenge, in England, are thought to have been inspired by astronomical events. But these people had no idea what the universe was made of, nor of its vast size. They thought of the Earth as flat, below a canopy of stars which revolved around the planet once a day.

THE PLACE OF THE EARTH
Most ancient Greeks believed that the Earth lay at the center of the universe. Ptolemy (A.D. 100–165), a great Greek astronomer, argued that the stars and planets must move around the Earth in circles, because the circle was a perfect shape created by the gods. His description of how the universe worked was accepted for more than 1,500 years.

ANCIENT DISCOVERIES
The Greek scholar Aristotle (384–322 B.C.) proved that the Earth must be round. He explained that when the Earth's shadow passes in front of the Moon during eclipses (see page 19), its edge appears to be curved, so it must be spherical in shape.

THE HEAVENLY SUN

The Sun has been worshiped as a god for thousands of years, by many different peoples. Ancient Hindus called the Sun-god Surya. He was one of the three main gods in their Holy Book of Divine Knowledge. In the fifth century B.C., ancient Greek religion linked the Sun to the god Apollo.

How many stars are there? With the naked eye, we can see about 2,000 stars on a clear night. But our galaxy alone contains 100,000 million stars. The entire universe probably contains at least a billion trillion stars – 1,000,000,000,000,000,000,000 of them!

LIGHTS IN THE SKY

Strange happenings in the skies caused fear and panic in ancient times, as they were believed to be omens of disaster. Comets frightened many people, while auroras, or natural displays of brightly colored lights, were believed to be angry gods.

Foretelling the future

Astrology is based on the ancient belief that the stars and planets control our lives. The signs of the zodiac represent the twelve constellations of stars through which the Sun appears to pass every year. An astrologer casts a horoscope from a person's date and place of birth. This predicts that person's future, based on the constellations.

THE CURVED EARTH

The Earth appeared flat, but Aristotle realized it was not. He knew that the number of stars you can see in the sky depends on where you are. The bright star Canopus can be seen from Egypt, but not from Greece. This would not happen if the Earth were flat.

HEAVENLY BLISS

The sky used to be seen as a solid canopy, not much higher than the highest mountains, with the stars set into it like jewels. Many religions believe that the heavens contain a better world to which good people go after they die, while those who have been bad in their lifetime are doomed to live underground.

Changing Views of
THE UNIVERSE

The first challenge to Ptolemy's Earth-centered universe came from Nicolaus Copernicus, in 1543. He realized that the movement of the planets was explained more easily if the Sun, not the Earth, lay at the center. But he did not dare publish his theories until the year of his death. Like Ptolemy, he believed that the planets moved in circles, but Johannes Kepler (1571-1630) showed that their orbits were elliptical (oval-shaped). To explain this, Isaac Newton (1643-1727) discovered the laws of gravity (the force which attracts objects toward each other). In the twentieth century, Albert Einstein's theories linked gravity, space, and time to explain the shape of the universe.

How big is the universe?
The universe is so big that light, which travels at 186,000 miles (300,000 km) per second, would take billions of years to reach us from its furthest edges.

REDRAWING THE UNIVERSE
Copernicus did not support Ptolemy's idea that all the stars circled the Earth once a day. He also realized that it could not explain all the movements of the Sun, Moon, and planets. His own theory declared the Earth an ordinary planet instead of the center of the universe.

THE PULL OF THE EARTH
Isaac Newton's theory of gravity applies equally to an apple falling from a tree and to the movement of the planets. He said that all objects are pulled together by a force based on their mass (the matter they contain) and their distance apart. This is why planets' orbits are elliptical.

EARLY OBSERVATIONS

Galileo used his telescope to confirm that Copernicus had been right to put the Sun at the center of the universe. The telescope was invented in 1608 by a Dutch  *eyeglass-maker, Hans Lippershey, who called it a "looker." He found that two lenses in a tube could magnify distant objects. When Galileo heard of this, he quickly built his own telescope, which he used to make many amazing discoveries.*

SEEING INTO SPACE

Tycho Brahe (1546–1601) was a Danish astronomer who built an observatory and kept precise records of the stars and planets. His assistant, Johannes Kepler (1571–1630), later used these records to show that the planets moved in elliptical (oval-shaped) orbits, rather than in circles.

A MODERN GENIUS

Albert Einstein (1879–1955) was one of the greatest physicists of the twentieth century. His theory combines space and time so that objects are given a position in time as well as in space. Gravity works by bending this space-time, making objects follow a curved path.

Fact or fiction?

Some of the most fantastic predictions of science fiction have come true. But so far we have not met aliens, or discovered a "warp drive" to travel at the speed of light. If Einstein was right, such speeds are impossible, so most of the universe will always be out of our reach.

"*As long as the Moon shall rise,*
As long as the rivers shall flow,
As long as the Sun shall shine,
As long as the grass shall grow."
Native American rhyme for treaties that
are meant to last forever.

The Solar SYSTEM

One star, nine planets, and a collection of asteroids, comets, and moons make up our solar system, the only part of the universe within range of modern spacecraft. Only the Earth has all the right conditions to have evolved into the planet we know. At the center of the solar system is the Sun, the star around which all the nine planets rotate. The planets lie in a flat, disklike shape, suggesting that they were formed from a disk of dust and gas spinning around the Sun. Most of the planets have their own moons: Earth and Pluto have one, Mars has two, Neptune eight, Uranus 15, Jupiter 16, and Saturn 18. Between the orbits of Mars and Jupiter there are more than 3,500 asteroids, or chunks of rock, ranging from 600 miles to less than 1 mile in diameter. There may be thousands of even smaller asteroids, which are too tiny to be seen from Earth. There may also be a tenth planet (Planet X) hidden beyond Pluto.

The Sun and its PLANETS

The Sun is the center and energy source of the solar system. It is over a million times the size of the Earth but only 330,000 times its mass, and consists mainly of the gases hydrogen and helium. Its energy comes from the hydrogen atoms joining together. At the Sun's surface, the temperature is 11,030°F , but in the center it is even hotter, at 30 million °F. The Earth orbits the Sun once a year, at a distance of about 93 million miles. In a spacecraft traveling at the top speed of a normal car, it would take 100 years to get from the Earth to the Sun!

THE POWERHOUSE OF THE SOLAR SYSTEM
Every second, the Sun converts four million tons of its gases into energy. At its surface, bursts of gas and energy leap out, called flares *and* prominences. *These produce so much energy that they can be felt on Earth as magnetic storms.*

WARNING: NEVER LOOK DIRECTLY AT THE SUN

Will the Sun ever run out of fuel?
Yes, but not for awhile. Every second, 600 million tons of hydrogen are changed into helium in the Sun. In about five billion years, the hydrogen will run out, the Sun will stop radiating energy, and all life on Earth will die.

Turn to page 4 for more facts about the planets.

THE DIVINE SUN
The Aztecs of Mexico and Central America believed that their world began when the gods sacrificed themselves to create the Sun. To help the Sun in its nightly battles with the Moon and stars, the Aztecs built huge temples, where they offered sacrifices and prayers.

THE INNER PLANETS

The four planets which are nearest to the Sun are Mercury, Venus, Earth, and Mars. These are made of rock and metal. They are often called the terrestrial planets because they are similar to the Earth.

Mercury	Venus	Earth	Mars

Mercury is small, bare, and so close to the Sun that its surface can reach temperatures up to 884°F. Venus is the planet nearest in size to the Earth, but it is very hot and is surrounded by clouds of sulfuric acid. Mars is covered with red rocks and dust, but is one of the few planets to have an atmosphere and frozen poles, like our North and South Poles.

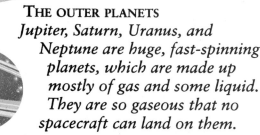

Naming the planets

The ancient Romans and Greeks knew only five planets – apart from the Earth – and gave them the names of their gods. Mercury was the Roman god of trade, Venus the goddess of love, and Mars the god of war. Jupiter controlled the weather, and Saturn was the father of the gods. The outer planets, discovered later, were also named after gods.

Uranus	Saturn	Jupiter

THE OUTER PLANETS

Jupiter, Saturn, Uranus, and Neptune are huge, fast-spinning planets, which are made up mostly of gas and some liquid. They are so gaseous that no spacecraft can land on them.

Neptune

Pluto

Pluto, however, is small, icy, and solid. Saturn, with its spectacular rings, is the most beautiful planet. The rings are more than 170,000 miles wide, but are only 60–100 feet thick, and consist of dust and chunks of ice orbiting the planet. Saturn is so light that it would float on water!

The Mysterious MOONS

The Moon, our nearest neighbor and the only object in space to which people have traveled, is just over 238,000 miles away – no distance at all in space! The Moon's cold light, its changing shape, and the markings on its surface have made it a fascinating object since the earliest times. Many ancient civilizations worshiped the Moon as a god. No other inner planet has a moon quite like ours: Mercury and Venus have no moons at all, and the two moons of Mars are tiny. The outer planets have so many moons that some remain to be discovered, but only four identified moons are bigger than our own.

The changing Moon
The Moon does not shine, but reflects sunlight. The changes of the Moon (phases) are due to the angles of the Earth, Sun, and Moon. With a new Moon, the side lit by the Sun faces away from the Earth. The Moon orbits, and more of the side facing the Earth is lit, until the Moon looks full.

"The Eagle has landed"
"The Eagle has landed"
On July 20, 1969, humans set foot on the Moon for the first time. The U.S. Apollo 11 spacecraft took Neil Armstrong, "Buzz" Aldrin, and Michael Collins to a landing in the Sea of Tranquility, and brought them safely home. By 1972, another ten people had visited the Moon, but nobody has been back since. The Apollo missions found that the Moon was a bare, cratered land, with rocks very much like those on Earth.

THE FACE OF OUR MOON
The Moon revolves in exactly the same time it takes to orbit the Earth, so it always shows us the same face. Its surface is pitted with craters caused by rocks crashing into it. Volcanoes have also shaped its surface, by pouring out molten lava to form pits or "seas" which never contained water. Throughout history, many peoples have thought they could see figures like rabbits within the Moon. In ancient Egyptian mythology, the Moon was believed to be the left eye of the god Horus.

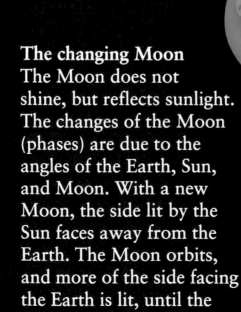

CHEESE FEAST

In the Middle Ages, some people believed that the Moon's surface was made of green cheese! We now know that it consists of finely-powdered rock.

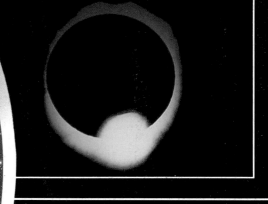

Shadows in space

Solar eclipses happen when the Sun, Moon, and Earth lie in a straight line. The Moon seems to block the Sun's light (below). Lunar eclipses occur when the Moon passes through the Earth's shadow. Ancient Chinese people believed that solar eclipses were dragons eating the Sun.

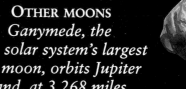

OTHER MOONS

Ganymede, the solar system's largest moon, orbits Jupiter and, at 3,268 miles (5,260 km) in diameter, is 1.5 times bigger than our Moon. Saturn's biggest moon, Titan, is the only moon with a thick atmosphere, which consists of nitrogen, methane, and cyanide. Titan may have oceans of liquid methane.

Where did the Moon come from? Nobody really knows. The most popular theory is that it was formed when a huge object from space collided with the Earth. The collision hurled up debris from the Earth to form a ring, which became the Moon. Another theory suggests that originally the Moon existed elsewhere in the solar system and was pulled toward the Earth by gravity. However, most scientists think that this is very unlikely.

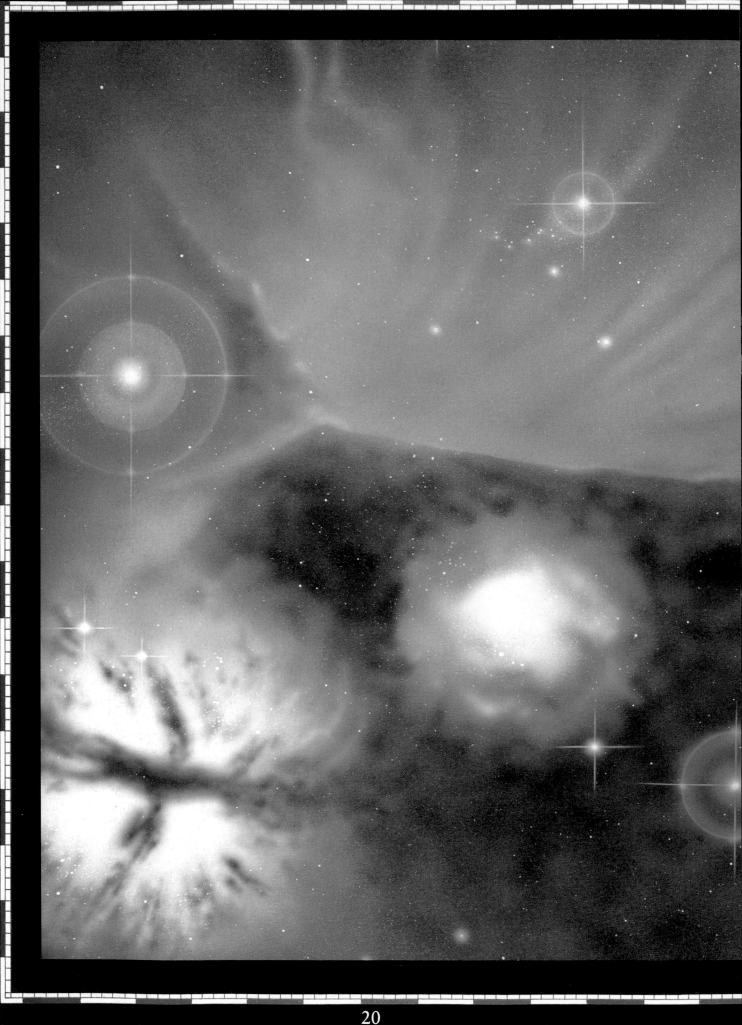

Stars and GALAXIES

The solar system is big, but it is tiny compared to the distances between the stars. They are so far away that even the most powerful telescope on Earth will not show them as more than points of light. The stars are not spread evenly throughout space, but are grouped into large clusters, or galaxies. Our own galaxy, the Milky Way, contains 100,000 million stars. Traveling at the speed of light, it would take more than four years to get to the nearest one, Proxima Centauri. At that speed we would reach our own star, the Sun, in just eight minutes. To get to Andromeda, the nearest galaxy outside the Milky Way, it would take 2.2 million years.

Stars vary in brightness, depending on how bright and how far away they are. The brightest, which can be seen with the naked eye, have their own names, and ancient people grouped them into constellations. The stars in a constellation appear close together, but this is not true – some are further away from the Earth than others.

"Awake! for Morning in the Bowl of Night
Has flung the Stone that turns the Stars to flight
And lo! The Hunter of the East has caught
The Sultan's Turret in a Noose of Light."
Omar Khayyam, Persian poet and astronomer (1048–1131), translated by Edward Fitzgerald

Comets and SHOOTING STARS

Comets were once believed to be stars. They used to strike fear into human beings, because their arrival was thought to announce some great event, such as the death of a ruler. We now know that comets are icy wanderers from the edges of the solar system, which swing close to the Sun every so often. They become visible as they are heated by the Sun, turning the ice into vapor which forms a tail. When the Earth passes through the dust left by a comet, the particles burn up in the atmosphere as meteors.

WHAT ARE COMETS?
Comets are dirty snowballs, ranging from the size of a house to a few miles across. They are made of soot, dust, and ice, and are much too small to see until they approach the Sun. As they get closer, the heat of the Sun turns the ice into steam, or vapor. This makes a glowing cloud and a long, glowing tail which always points away from the Sun and streams behind the comet as it journeys across the sky. At this stage it is possible to see the comet from the Earth. Scientists think that there might be millions of comets traveling through space.

A regular visitor
The most famous comet of all is Halley's Comet, which reappears every 76 years. It was named by the eighteenth-century astronomer Edmund Halley. In 1986, the comet was examined by the Giotto spacecraft. Comet Hale-Bopp was clearly visible in 1997, but will not return for 4,000 years.

COMETS IN HISTORY

Comet sightings have been recorded since ancient times. It may have been a comet, not a star, that appeared at the birth of Christ, as told in the Bible. The medieval Bayeux Tapestry in France shows people marveling at Halley's Comet, which made one of its appearances in 1066.

How many shooting stars are there? Every day, 300 tons of dust and rock fall into the Earth's atmosphere. Almost all of this consists of tiny particles that burn up, forming meteors. Millions of particles hit the planet every day, but most of them are so tiny that an observer on Earth will see only about 10 shooting stars per hour.

DRAGONS IN THE SKY

Meteorites are chunks of rock from the asteroids in the solar system. They are too big to burn up when they enter the Earth's atmosphere, and hit the ground. They are clearly visible in the sky, and can be terrifying. Meteorites have frightened people throughout history. They were often believed to be huge, fiery dragons coming to attack the world, or weapons of revenge sent by the angry gods to destroy the Earth.

COLLISION

In July 1994, the comet Shoemaker-Levy 9 collided with the planet Jupiter. It was broken into more than 20 pieces before impact, but it still left huge craters.

CRASH!

When a huge meteorite landed near Tunguska, Siberia, in 1908 (below), it destroyed the surrounding forests for miles, leaving the landscape desolate and ruined. Luckily, nobody was hurt.

ARE WE IN DANGER?

About 50,000 years ago, a large meteorite hit Arizona, making a vast crater. If a really huge meteorite hit Earth, its effect might be deadly.

The Starry SKIES

Like human beings, stars are born, grow old, and die. If we look hard enough, we can find stars of every age in the sky. Stars are formed from clouds of hydrogen gas collapsing under the force of gravity and turning into helium gas, in a process that produces huge amounts of energy. Near the end of the lives of giant stars, the helium changes into even heavier substances. Eventually these giant stars blow up in huge explosions called supernovae, scattering elements like carbon, silicon, iron, and oxygen into space. New stars and planets form from this debris. The Earth and everything in it, including ourselves, is in fact made of recycled material from a long-dead star.

GIANTS AND DWARFS
The biggest stars, or "red giants," have a lot of pressure in their core, burn quickly and brightly and die earliest, leaving the core as a "white dwarf." Tiny, dim stars, or "brown dwarfs," never become true stars. They get gradually fainter, and finally fade into "black dwarfs."

Into the void
After a huge star explodes, the core is left behind and collapses into a tiny point – a black hole. The pull of gravity from a black hole is so strong that not even light can escape from it.

THE LIFE OF A STAR
A star like the Sun begins as a cloud of gas and dust, which is gradually squashed by the force of gravity to make the star. At the end of its life it swells up into a "red giant" star, then puffs off its outer layers of gas into space. Even our Sun will finally end its life as a tiny "white dwarf" star.

A SCIENTIFIC BREAKTHROUGH
Sir Arthur Eddington (1882–1944) was the first person to realize that the mysterious spiral shapes seen in the sky were galaxies. He also proved that Einstein's theory of gravity was correct, by watching light being bent during an eclipse in 1919. Eddington wrote several famous books that explained the nature of the universe in a simple, understandable way.

OUR OWN GALAXY

The Milky Way is a spiral-shaped galaxy. Our solar system is on one of the "arms" of the galaxy, about two-thirds of the way out.

STAR PULSES

Super-dense stars called neutron stars, which measure about 20 miles across, spin quickly and send out radio signals. The regular pulses picked up from these stars by large radio receivers on Earth give them the name pulsars.

PATTERNS IN SPACE

Galaxies form in four different shapes. Spiral galaxies are like pinwheels, and the oldest stars are contained in elliptical (oval-shaped) galaxies. Barred spiral galaxies have a thick line running through the middle. Other galaxies have irregular shapes, depending on the number of stars and their position in space.

What would happen if I fell feet first into a black hole?

You would be stretched out like a piece of spaghetti, because the force at your feet would be stronger than that at your head. Then you would disappear beyond the "event horizon." Nothing, not even light, can escape from the black hole once it has passed this point.

THE BRIGHTEST STAR

Eta Carinae is the most luminous known star of all. It is 150 times bigger than the Sun, and six million times brighter.

THE CONSTELLATIONS

There are 88 identified constellations in the universe. Each has its own area of the sky, decided in 1930. The constellations are useful for finding your way around the sky.

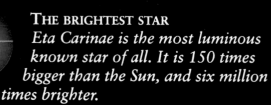

Exploring the
UNIVERSE

Our knowledge of the universe depends on observation – through telescopes, radio telescopes, and satellites. The universe is so vast that we can never hope to travel far beyond the edges of the solar system. But many amazing things can be discovered simply by looking at our universe. We can tell what stars are made of, how far away they are, how fast they are moving, and how hot, bright, or old they are. By putting telescopes on the tops of mountains, we can see much further and much more clearly than at ground level, because there is less air and pollution to look through, and therefore the image is clearer. Telescopes in space, such as the Hubble telescope, work even better, and produce incredibly clear pictures. Nearly 400 years of observation through telescopes have shown that the universe is indeed mysterious, and that there must be many strange things waiting to be discovered.

"My own suspicion is that the universe is not only queerer than we suppose, but queerer than we can suppose."
J.B.S. Haldane

Observing the UNIVERSE

Bigger telescopes work better than smaller ones, because they collect more light and can detect dimmer and more distant objects. However, if lenses are too big they can be so heavy that they bend, making the image less accurate. Curved mirrors work better because they reflect the light and therefore can be supported from behind. Electronic devices can be used to collect and record results more accurately than the human eye. But even the most powerful telescopes on Earth cannot show all the details of a distant star or the planets orbiting it.

THE FIRST TELESCOPES

Galileo's telescope, built in 1609, consisted of two lenses mounted at either end of a tube. By 1671, Isaac Newton had invented a reflecting telescope that used mirrors. In 1845, the Earl of Rosse built a 72-inch (180-cm) reflecting telescope, with which he discovered the spiral shape of some galaxies. In 1931, Karl Jansky accidentally discovered radio waves coming from the Milky Way. These inspired Grote Reber to invent the first radio telescope in 1936, which allowed astronomers to explore the universe in greater detail.

OBSERVATORIES

Highly polluted cities such as Los Angeles and London are too dirty for a good, clear view of the stars. Therefore, more remote spots have been found. The best modern observatories are on mountains in Hawaii and the Canary Islands, and similar areas with clear, clean skies.

The U.S. Orbiting Solar Observatory satellites are the primary astronomical observatories in space. The first was launched in 1962.

A pioneering vision

The Hubble space telescope, launched in 1990, has a 94-inch (235-cm) reflector and orbits 370 miles (618 km) above the Earth. Repaired in 1993, new instruments were added by a servicing mission in 1997. Hubble is sending back the clearest pictures of distant objects ever taken.

Which is the biggest telescope in the world? The biggest telescope is the Keck 33-foot (10-m) reflector at Mauna Kea in Hawaii. The mirror's measurements are accurate to within one-thousandth of the width of a human hair.

RADIO WAVES

Radio telescopes are used to listen to radio signals given out by stars and galaxies. They may be either big dishes designed to collect the radio waves, or simple aerials. Their signals are combined by computers. The result is not a picture but a graph, which can then be converted into an image. Several widely-spaced radio telescopes can be linked and their signals combined, to produce an accurate, detailed description of a single radio source in space.

Karl Jansky

BEYOND SIGHT

The light we see from stars is only a tiny fraction of the energy they give out. Telescopes – some of them positioned in space – can be designed to collect other kinds of waves, including infrared and ultraviolet rays (invisible light rays), X rays, and gamma rays.

Fantastic VOYAGES

With the development of the rocket, people's dreams of space travel finally came true. Rockets burn fuel to produce gases that escape through a nozzle, causing the rocket to thrust forward. Their engines are the only kind that can work in space, and they must carry all their fuel and oxygen to burn it. The secret of reaching space is the multi-stage rocket, in which various parts burn out and fall off, one after another. Since the first rockets went into space, spacecraft have explored the solar system to its very limits, and people have walked on the Moon.

A VISION OF THE FUTURE
The French author Jules Verne was well known for his futuristic visions. In 1865 he wrote a book about a journey to the Moon. His space travelers were fired from a gun – which in real life would have killed them – and had to fly around the Moon, and then come back, because they had no way of landing.

THE ROCKET PIONEERS
The principles of rocketry were developed by Konstantin Tsiolkovsky, a Russian teacher, at the beginning of the twentieth century. Robert Goddard, an American physicist whose early rocket is shown bottom left, and Werner von Braun (above) from Germany went on to build and launch successful rockets. Von Braun's V-2 rocket (top left) was used by the Nazis as a devastating weapon during the last year of World War II (1939–1945).

NASA
The National Aeronautics and Space Administration (NASA) put the first person on the Moon in July 1969. But unstaffed NASA missions to the planets have taught us more. For example, the Mars Pathfinder landed on July 4 1997 and found no signs of life on the planet.

Can we make time stand still?
If we can ever design a spacecraft that is able to travel at the speed of light, time on board will stand still, according to Albert Einstein's theories. An astronaut could travel for 1,000 years and come back no older than the day he or she set off. But it is unlikely that technology will ever develop enough to build such a fast craft.

ALONE IN SPACE

The first person in space, Major Yuri Gagarin, was launched by the former Soviet Union in Vostok 1 on April 12, 1961. He completed a single orbit of the Earth, and landed safely.

PROBING DEEP SPACE

The first space probes to leave the solar system were Pioneer 10 and 11, then two Voyager spacecraft. The Voyager craft took closeup pictures of Jupiter and Saturn in 1979, then Voyager 2 went on to visit Uranus and Neptune. Galileo reached Jupiter in 1995, and has sent back amazing information on Jupiter and its moons.

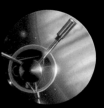

LITTER-BUGS

The landscapes of the solar system are dotted with equipment left behind by various expeditions.

EARTH'S CALLING CARD

Pioneer 10, which was launched in 1972, carries a plaque of information, or "calling card," in case it should ever meet other intelligent life. It has a diagram showing what human beings look like, and a sky map to identify where our solar system is.

The Future of the UNIVERSE

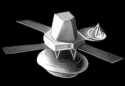

> "We find ourselves in a bewildering world. We want to make sense of what we see around us and to ask: What is the nature of the universe? What is our place in it and where did it and we come from? Why is it the way it is?"
> Stephen Hawking,
> *A Brief History of Time*

Nearly all astronomers believe that the universe began with a big bang. About 15 billion years ago, the universe was incredibly hot and very small – even smaller than an atom. Then it began to expand at a very fast rate. Today, everything in the universe is still moving apart. Various recent discoveries have provided strong evidence that this theory is correct.

If the universe began with a big bang, how will it end? That is much more uncertain. It may go on expanding forever, or it may stop expanding, start shrinking, and eventually end in a big crunch sometime in the distant future. It all depends on how much material the universe contains. If there is enough material, the pull of its gravity will be strong enough to stop the universe from expanding and eventually make it collapse in a big crunch. Of course, this wouldn't happen for millions of years!

Is There Anybody OUT THERE?

Are we alone in our universe? If life evolved (developed) naturally on Earth, as most scientists believe, it has probably evolved somewhere else too. There are so many billions of stars similar to the Sun that many of them must have planets. Among those planets there might be some with conditions like those on Earth. If so, then we are almost certainly not alone. To find other intelligent life, we must constantly listen and observe. For more than 30 years, radio telescopes have been pointed at the stars to try to pick up any radio signals from distant civilizations – but so far without success. The search for life in our universe goes on, and may continue forever.

HAVE WE MET BEFORE?
Mysterious lines are clearly visible across the desert in Peru, and are thought by some people to be the work of ancient aliens.

A LONG HISTORY
Throughout history, strange, unknown lights in the sky have made people wonder about other life in the universe.

LIFE ON MARS?
The astronomer Percival Lowell (1855–1916) believed that he could see canals on Mars, evidence of intelligent life there. But these were optical illusions, as photographs by the Viking spacecraft proved.

LIGHTS IN THE SKY
Many people have seen strange, disk-shaped objects in the sky. These have been named Unidentified Flying Objects, *or UFOs. But in spite of many rumors and continuous observation of the skies, there is no hard evidence that they are alien spacecraft. Most UFOs are probably oddly-shaped clouds, or have been cleverly faked in photographs.*

Is there proof of life in other galaxies? In 1995, British ufologists (people who study UFOs) claimed that they had seen a U.S. government film from 1947. They claimed it showed scientists examining the body of an alien whose craft crashed in New Mexico. Could this solve one of the greatest mysteries of our universe?

THE FACE OF MARS

Lowell's theories of Martian life were proved wrong, but years later, a picture taken by a Viking probe seemed to show a face carved on the planet's surface.

Was this evidence of an ancient Martian civilization? Unfortunately not. The human eye is so good at recognizing faces that it can easily trick the brain into thinking it can see one – in a rock of roughly the right shape or a landscape covered with shadows, for example.

Little green men?

Most images of aliens have been created in films such as *E.T.* Aliens are often shown as green or gray in color, have large eyes, and talk slowly and carefully. A real alien would probably be quite different, and might think that we look really weird. Or it might look exactly the same as a human!

A NATIONAL ALERT

The War of the Worlds, *by the English writer H.G. Wells, describes an invasion of the Earth by Martians.*

The novel was written in England in 1898, and was turned into a radio play in 1938. When it was broadcast, the story was so convincing that thousands of listeners thought it was a real news bulletin, and ran screaming into the streets in their pajamas. Many other futuristic novels have since been written, but none had such a dramatic effect!

The Unsolved MYSTERIES

The greatest unsolved mystery of the universe is how much of it there is. Spiral galaxies keep their shape so well that they must contain far more material than we can see. In fact, visible stars make up probably only about one-tenth of the total mass (material) of the universe. So what makes up the rest, or the "missing mass?" It might be stars that are too dim to see, but in fact we just don't know. It is important to find the answer because the mass determines whether the universe will go on expanding forever, ending cold and empty in a big chill, or whether it will eventually shrink into nothingness during a big crunch.

TIME TRAVEL
In films, such as Dr. Who (top) or Back to the Future (left), and books like The Time Machine (right), people travel through time, but will this ever be possible? Einstein's Theory of Relativity suggests that somebody falling into a black hole would not be killed, but might pass through "wormholes" to reach another universe, another part of our universe, or another time.

WORMING THROUGH SPACE
Wormholes are tunnels that link one part of space-time with another. If space-time is curved like the surface of an apple, then a wormhole is like a shortcut to the other side, through which objects might be able to travel from one time to another. It sounds crazy – but it could be true.

The Big Crunch
Many scientists believe that the universe will eventually end as it started – as a single point. If this big crunch does occur, what will happen to the universe next? The whole process might start again with another big bang, to form new stars, planets, and galaxies – and a new Earth?

How many black holes are there? There could be more black holes than the number of visible stars – that is, more than a hundred billion in our galaxy alone. If so, they would account for a lot of the "missing mass" in space, because black holes can contain enough material to make 100,000 suns.

DEADLY IMPACT

Sixty-five million years ago, a huge asteroid hit the Earth, making a cloud of debris that changed the climate, killing the dinosaurs. It could happen again. Astronomers are watching, to give us warning.

PLANET X
Deep in the solar system, there could be a tenth planet. So far, searches for Planet X have failed, but the hunt continues...

COLONIZING MARS
Mars is the only planet close to being able to support life. If it was artificially heated over many centuries, it could perhaps be a new Earth.

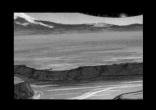

Looking to the future

Our universe was created 15 billion years ago, yet human life has only existed for a tiny fraction of that time. It will take hundreds, perhaps thousands of years for us to come even close to understanding all the secrets of space. With so many new worlds and galaxies to explore and so many questions to answer, it is no wonder that scientists and other people are forever trying to unravel the mysteries of the universe.

TIME LINE

4th century B.C. *Aristotle shows that Earth is round*

240 B.C. *First recorded sighting of Halley's Comet*

2nd century A.D. *Ptolemy creates theory of the universe*

1543 *Copernicus asserts his theory of the solar system*
1572 *Brahe observes stars and planets*

1600 *Kepler shows planets move in elliptical orbits*
1610 *January 7, Galileo sees Jupiter's moons*
1671 *Newton invents reflecting telescope*
1675 *Royal Greenwich Observatory founded*

1807 *Rockets used during Napoleonic War*
1845 *Earl of Rosse builds 72-inch reflecting telescope*
1865 *Verne's* From the Earth to the Moon
1898 *Wells'* The War of the Worlds

1903 *Tsiolkovsky works out basic principles of space flight*

1914 *Eddington identifies spiral galaxies*
1915-1916 *Einstein publishes Theory of Relativity*

1923 *Oberth publishes book on space flight*
1926 *Goddard launches first liquid-propellant rocket*

1930 *Pluto discovered*
1931 *Jansky finds radio waves in space*
1936 *Reber builds radio telescope*

1942 *V-2 rocket reaches height of 150 miles*

1957 *October 4, Soviet satellite Sputnik 1 launched*
        November: Launch of Sputnik 2, with dog Laika
1958 *January 31, U.S. satellite Explorer 1 launched*
        July: NASA created
1959 *Soviet Luna 3 probe photographs far side of Moon for first time*
1960 *February: First weather satellite, TIROS 1, launched*
        Soviet SS-7 rocket explodes on launchpad, killing many people
        First U.S. deep space probe, Pioneer 5, launched
1961 *April 12, Cosmonaut Yuri Gagarin makes single orbit of Earth*
        May: Alan Shephard is first American in space
        August: Cosmonaut Gherman Titov orbits Earth 16 times
1962 *John Glenn is first American to orbit Earth*

April: U.S. probe Ranger 4 strikes Moon
April 26 British satellite Ariel 1 is launched
Mariner 2 probe visits Venus
July: Telstar communications satellite launched
1963 Cosmonaut Valentina Tereshkova is first woman in space
1964 Soviet Union puts 3 people into orbit in Voshkod 1
1965 March: NASA's first staffed Gemini flight
Alexsei Leonov makes first space walk from Voshkod 2
July: U.S. probe Mariner 4 photographs Mars
1966 January: Soviet probe Luna 9 lands on Moon
1967 Three Apollo astronauts killed in a launchpad fire
June: Soviet probe Venera 4 transmits data on Venus
Pulsars discovered
1968 October: First manned Apollo flight
December: Three astronauts orbit Moon in Apollo 8
1969 July 20, Apollo 11 lands on Moon

1971 December: Capsule from Soviet probe, Mars 3, lands on Mars
November: NASA's probe, Mariner 9, is first to orbit Mars
1972 Pioneer 10 launched, carrying "calling card"
1973 May: Skylab 2 launched with crew of three
1975 July: US Apollo and Soviet Soyuz spacecraft link in space
October: Soviet probe Venera 9 lands on Venus
1976 Viking 1 sends photographs from Mars
1977 NASA launches Voyagers 1 and 2

1981 April: First flight of U.S. space
shuttle Columbia
1983 June: Pioneer 10 travels
beyond all planets November:
Spacelab, built by European
Space Agency (ESA), launched
1986 January: Challenger space
shuttle explodes
February: Launch of Mir
space station

March: Giotto photographs Halley's Comet
1988 November: launch of Buran shuttle

1990 Hubble space telescope launched
1992 Shuttle astronauts make eight-hour space
walk
1994 July: Comet Shoemaker-Levy collides
with Jupiter
1995 Galileo reaches Jupiter
1997 Comet Hale-Bopp is clearly visible
1997 July: Mars Pathfinder lands on Mars
deploying a rover, Sojourner.
1998 November: First part of International Space Station assembled in space.
2000 May: US shuttle mission to International Space Station

INDEX

Picture Credits: 4-5, 19, 28 both: Science Photo Library; 13 both: Mary Evans Picture Library; 30: Nasa; 34, 35: Frank Spooner Pictures.